1

Dedicated to:

- All who wish to awaken their inner JOY.

- All who wish to attract more of the vibrational energy they want, into their life.

- All who wish to find appreciation in the "moments" and the "now" in their life.

Other Publications by this Author:
The Voyage: Finding the Beautiful Gems of My Being
The Voyage: All Age Coloring Book
Volume 1- Positive Quotes with Author Holly
Volume 2- Positive Quotes with Author Holly
90 day Gratitude/JOY Pocket Journal
90 day Daily Self-Care Accountability Logbook
90 day Daily Self-Care Accountability Log/ Reflect Journal
30 day Daily Self-Care Accountability Logbook
Volume 3- Positive Quotes with Author Holly
30 day Daily Self-Care Accountability Log/ Reflect Journal

Joyful Navigations

30 day

Gratitude/JOY

Pocket Journal

Holly Ruttenbur Dickinson

30 day Gratitude/JOY Pocket Journal
by Holly Ruttenbur Dickinson.

A 30 day Gratitude/JOY Pocket Journal .

Copyright ©2020 Holly Ruttenbur Dickinson
Joyful Navigations/Trade Name
Joyful Navigations™
Published by Shifting Open LLC.

Self-Help, Personal Growth, Happiness, Success,
Motivational, Gratitude, Joy, Joyful, Journaling

Book Design, Graphics, Journaling Design by Holly
Dickinson

Printed in the United States of America

ISBN: 978-1-7355347-2-5

Table of Contents

A daily GRATITUDE journal brings me into the present moment and reminds me of all the most simple things I have to be grateful for. This is self-care. It reminds me of my JOY.

Focusing on gratitude daily, has literally rewired my brain to GO TO THE GRATITUDE. And in that gratitude, is MY JOY. It's been such a beautiful process of self discovery.

JOY and GRATITUDE are so interwoven that's it's near impossible to separate them.

When GRATITUDE is my daily practice, everything has a brighter side to it.

More gratitude, less complaining. If you don't like something, work to make it better instead. Complaining attracts more of the energy of what you don't want. Gratitude attracts more of the energy of what you want.

A daily gratitude practice isn't about denying or ignoring your other feelings and emotions or ignoring situations that need to be changed because they aren't working. Each is important to recognize and validate. A daily gratitude practice shouldn't be forced or for an external benefit accept your own well being. Willingly shifting one's focus, allows one to center on the good parts of their life, their BE-ingness. And the more JOY one receives from those simple JOYS, the more driven one can be to make the non-working parts of their life better as well.

Suggested Gratitude Process

- Keep the pocket journal next to your bed or where you do your wake up self-care routine. Or Keep it in your day bag where it can be close to your fingertips for quick access during times of the day you know you will be able to write.

- Allow the daily practice to be a priority in order to shift your mindset to be more positive and happier. Allow your feelings in.

- No need to start at the beginning of a month. Start whenever you want throughout the month. The date is left blank for you to fill in on your schedule. The more often you do this as a daily routine, the faster it will become a healthy self-care habit. If you miss a day, that is ok. Just pick up the following day and resume the routine.

- On the "Gratitude/JOY" line, write general words. Example: Today's taxi driver.On the "Expand" lines, simply expand on your thought of why you are grateful for what you wrote as your general word/s. Example: "Grateful for today's taxi driver because she had a kind personality and was respectful. We got into a nice conversation and it helped set my day off right. I noticed that I was treating people at work kindly as well. It felt good."

Date _____   Day 1

Gratitude/JOY_____

Expand_____

_____

_____

_____

_____

_____

_____

_____

_____

_____

_____

_____

_____

_____

_____

_____

_____

Date _____ Day 2

Gratitude/JOY_____

Expand_____

_____

_____

_____

_____

_____

_____

_____

_____

_____

_____

_____

_____

_____

_____

_____

_____

Date _____   Day 3

Gratitude/JOY_____

Expand_____

_____

_____

_____

_____

_____

_____

_____

_____

_____

_____

_____

_____

_____

_____

_____

_____

_____

_____

Date _____   Day 4

Gratitude/JOY_____

Expand_____

_____

_____

_____

_____

_____

_____

_____

_____

_____

_____

_____

_____

_____

_____

_____

_____

Date _____ Day 5

Gratitude/JOY_____

Expand_____

_____

_____

_____

_____

_____

_____

_____

_____

_____

_____

_____

_____

_____

_____

_____

_____

_____

Date _____ Day 6

Gratitude/JOY_____

Expand_____
_____
_____
_____
_____
_____
_____
_____
_____
_____
_____
_____
_____
_____
_____
_____
_____
_____
_____
_____

Date _____ Day 7

Gratitude/JOY_____

Expand_____

_____

_____

_____

_____

_____

_____

_____

_____

_____

_____

_____

_____

_____

_____

_____

Date _____ Day 8

Gratitude/JOY_____

Expand_____

_____

_____

_____

_____

_____

_____

_____

_____

_____

_____

_____

_____

_____

_____

_____

_____

_____

Date _____   Day 9

Gratitude/JOY_____

Expand_____
_____
_____
_____
_____
_____
_____
_____
_____
_____
_____
_____
_____
_____
_____
_____
_____
_____
_____

Date _____   Day 10

Gratitude/JOY_____

Expand_____
_____
_____
_____
_____
_____
_____
_____
_____
_____
_____
_____
_____
_____
_____
_____
_____
_____
_____

Date _____ Day 11

Gratitude/JOY_____

Expand_____

_____

_____

_____

_____

_____

_____

_____

_____

_____

_____

_____

_____

_____

_____

_____

_____

_____

Date _____   Day 12

Gratitude/JOY_____

Expand_____
_____
_____
_____
_____
_____
_____
_____
_____
_____
_____
_____
_____
_____
_____
_____
_____
_____
_____

Date _____ Day 13

Gratitude/JOY_____

Expand_____

_____

_____

_____

_____

_____

_____

_____

_____

_____

_____

_____

_____

_____

_____

_____

_____

Date _____   Day 14

Gratitude/JOY_____

Expand_____

_____

_____

_____

_____

_____

_____

_____

_____

_____

_____

_____

_____

_____

_____

_____

_____

_____

Date _____   Day 15

Gratitude/JOY_____

Expand_____
_____
_____
_____
_____
_____
_____
_____
_____
_____
_____
_____
_____
_____
_____
_____
_____
_____
_____
_____

Date _____   Day 16

Gratitude/JOY_____

Expand_____

_____

_____

_____

_____

_____

_____

_____

_____

_____

_____

_____

_____

_____

_____

_____

_____

_____

Date _____ Day 17

Gratitude/JOY_____

Expand_____

_____

_____

_____

_____

_____

_____

_____

_____

_____

_____

_____

_____

_____

_____

_____

_____

Date _____   Day 18

Gratitude/JOY_____

Expand_____

_____

_____

_____

_____

_____

_____

_____

_____

_____

_____

_____

_____

_____

_____

_____

_____

_____

Date _____ Day 19

Gratitude/JOY_____

Expand_____

_____

_____

_____

_____

_____

_____

_____

_____

_____

_____

_____

_____

_____

_____

_____

_____

_____

Date _____ Day 20

Gratitude/JOY_____

Expand_____

_____

_____

_____

_____

_____

_____

_____

_____

_____

_____

_____

_____

_____

_____

_____

_____

Date _____ Day 21

Gratitude/JOY_____

Expand_____
_____
_____
_____
_____
_____
_____
_____
_____
_____
_____
_____
_____
_____
_____
_____
_____
_____
_____

Date _____ Day 22

Gratitude/JOY_____

Expand_____
_____
_____
_____
_____
_____
_____
_____
_____
_____
_____
_____
_____
_____
_____
_____
_____
_____

Date _____ Day 23

Gratitude/JOY_____

Expand_____
_____
_____
_____
_____
_____
_____
_____
_____
_____
_____
_____
_____
_____
_____
_____
_____

Date _____ Day 24

Gratitude/JOY_____

Expand_____
_____
_____
_____
_____
_____
_____
_____
_____
_____
_____
_____
_____
_____
_____
_____
_____
_____
_____

Date _____ Day 25

Gratitude/JOY_____

Expand_____

_____

_____

_____

_____

_____

_____

_____

_____

_____

_____

_____

_____

_____

_____

_____

_____

_____

Date _____   Day 26

Gratitude/JOY_____

Expand_____

_____

_____

_____

_____

_____

_____

_____

_____

_____

_____

_____

_____

_____

_____

_____

_____

Date _____ Day 27

Gratitude/JOY_____

Expand_____

_____

_____

_____

_____

_____

_____

_____

_____

_____

_____

_____

_____

_____

_____

_____

_____

_____

Date _____   Day 28

Gratitude/JOY_____

Expand_____

_____
_____
_____
_____
_____
_____
_____
_____
_____
_____
_____
_____
_____
_____
_____
_____
_____

Date _____   Day 29

Gratitude/JOY_____

Expand_____
_____
_____
_____
_____
_____
_____
_____
_____
_____
_____
_____
_____
_____
_____
_____
_____
_____

Date _____   Day 30

Gratitude/JOY_____

Expand_____

_____

_____

_____

_____

_____

_____

_____

_____

_____

_____

_____

_____

_____

_____

_____

_____

Date _____

Gratitude/JOY_____

Expand_____

_____

_____

_____

_____

_____

_____

_____

_____

_____

_____

_____

_____

_____

_____

_____

_____

_____

Date _____

Gratitude/JOY_____

Expand_____

_____

_____

_____

_____

_____

_____

_____

_____

_____

_____

_____

_____

_____

_____

_____

_____

_____

Notes

_____

_____

_____

_____

_____

_____

_____

_____

_____

_____

_____

_____

_____

_____

_____

_____

_____

_____

Notes

_____

_____

_____

_____

_____

_____

_____

_____

_____

_____

_____

_____

_____

_____

_____

_____

_____

Notes

_____

_____

_____

_____

_____

_____

_____

_____

_____

_____

_____

_____

_____

_____

_____

_____

_____

_____

_____

Notes

_____
_____
_____
_____
_____
_____
_____
_____
_____
_____
_____
_____
_____
_____
_____
_____
_____
_____

A Message from the Author

Words can barely express how the daily practice of gratitude has positively altered my life. I think it would be a challenge for anyone to truly understand this until they experience the change, the shift, in their own life. I had heard that gratitude could change one's life and could attract more positive energy into one's life. I wanted to test the theory. I wanted to know if it was true. And so I took a 365 day gratitude/JOY journey. I allowed my life to be my own test subject. Within the first 30 days I began to notice more happiness and joy in my attitude and my whole being with the daily practice of gratitude. I started each day off with it and many nights I would do a second round. Imagine a year of this routine which became a very healthy self-care habit. Gratitude takes you out of "what's wrong" thinking and into "what's right" thinking in your life. May you dedicate yourself to a more JOYful life through gratitude. ~Author Holly, Your Joyful Guide.

Visit me on the Facebook Page: *Positive Quotes with Author Holly* and *Choose Joyful with Joyful Navigations*™

Website: https://joyfulnavigations.com

About the Author

Author Holly R. Dickinson is a Lightworker and a Mass Influencer of 7 million plus followers on her Facebook Page. She is a Mother of 4, now adults. She is in a loving marriage to her husband of 27 years. Early life brought many traumas and challenges to her. She shares her wisdom, perspectives, and courage in her writings. God, love, kindness, gratitude, family, awareness, courage, action, trust, compassion, forgiveness, self-care, positivity, and choosing joy are key for her.